THE INFLUENCE FORMULA

MAXWELL MOMENTS

THE INFLUENCE FORMULA

4 STEPS TO HELP YOU LEAD ANYONE WELL

JOHN C. MAXWELL

CENTER STREET

Nashville • New York

The author is represented by Yates & Yates, LLP, Literary Agency, Santa Ana, California.

Center Street
Hachette Book Group
1290 Avenue of the Americas, New York, NY 10104
centerstreet.com
twitter.com/centerstreet

First Edition: January 2023

Center Street is a division of Hachette Book Group, Inc. The Center Street name and logo are trademarks of Hachette Book Group, Inc.

The publisher is not responsible for websites (or their content) that are not owned by the publisher.

The Hachette Speakers Bureau provides a wide range of authors for speaking events. To find out more, go to www.HachetteSpeakersBureau.com or call (866) 376-6591.

Print book interior design by Bart Dawson.

Library of Congress Cataloging-in-Publication Data
Names: Maxwell, John C., 1947- author.
Title: The influence formula : 4 steps to help you lead anyone well / John C. Maxwell.
Description: First edition. | Nashville : Center Street, 2023.
Identifiers: LCCN 2022037039 | ISBN 9781546002529 (trade paperback) | ISBN 9781546002536 (ebook)
Subjects: LCSH: Social influence. | Influence (Psychology) | Leadership.
Classification: LCC HM1176 .M48 2023 | DDC 302/.13--dc23/eng/20220902
LC record available at https://lccn.loc.gov/2022037039

ISBNs: 9781546002529 (paperback), 9781546002536 (ebook)

Printed in the United States of America

LSC-C

Printing 1, 2022

CONTENTS

LEADERSHIP REQUIRES INFLUENCE   1

STEP 1
PROVE YOURSELF   20

STEP 2
EARN RELATIONSHIPS   48

STEP 3
MAKE YOUR TEAM SUCCESSFUL   88

STEP 4
HELP PEOPLE REACH THEIR POTENTIAL   134

WITH GREAT INFLUENCE COMES GREAT RESPONSIBILITY   191
ACKNOWLEDGMENTS   202

LEADERSHIP REQUIRES INFLUENCE

If you want to lead another person,
you need influence.

But what is influence, really?
And how can you develop it?

Influence is creating a desire
in another person to act.

There was a time when people relied less on influence and more on position or title to lead others. That's no surprise, since at one time hereditary leadership positions were handed down from one generation to another. **Princes became kings, and their decisions were law—for good or for bad.**

Those days are gone. And we are better for it.

Today you must *earn* influence. Fewer people act out of duty. Or obligation. Or coercion. People do what they want.

The question is:

Do they want to follow you?

Even if you possess a title or *position* of authority, you still need influence to lead people. **Any position you have is little more than a starting place, a chance to earn influence.**

When you join the army, you become a recruit and must earn rank and the respect of your fellow soldiers.

When you land a job, you may receive a title or a job description: laborer, salesperson, waiter, clerk, accountant, manager. **But you must prove yourself.**

When you have children, you have the position and title of parent. But the older your children get, the more you need influence if you want to help them grow into happy, healthy, productive adults.

"ALL THE LETTERS BEFORE OR AFTER A NAME ARE LIKE THE TAIL ON A PIG. IT HAS NOTHING TO DO WITH THE QUALITY OF THE BACON."

—Claude Winninger

Developing influence is both art and science. Some people influence others naturally. They have so much charisma, **personality,** beauty, or talent that people want to follow them.

But you don't need to possess those things to develop influence or lead others. You can follow a formula:

- Prove yourself.

- Earn relationships.

- Make your team successful.

- Help people reach their potential.

Does the word *formula* sound cold or impersonal? It doesn't have to. You're not going to treat people as numbers or objects. You're just taking the right steps in the right order. With each step, you help others. At the same time, you accomplish the tasks needed to gain influence with the people you're working with.

This is how you gain influence. This is a formula anyone can follow. If you earn influence with someone, then you can lead them.

"NO MAN IS A LEADER
UNTIL HIS APPOINTMENT
IS RATIFIED IN THE MINDS
AND THE HEARTS OF HIS MEN."

—Infantryman's journal (1954)

Don't think of *influence* as a noun, something that's been completed. Think of *influence* as a verb. It's active. It's ongoing. **It's something you must do every day with the people you desire to lead.**

"SHOW ME WHAT YOU CAN DO;
DON'T TELL ME WHAT YOU CAN DO!"

—John Wooden

As an active influencer, you never arrive. Neither do the people you're leading. **Good leaders are always working to take people somewhere worthwhile.** They aren't static. If there is no journey, there is no leadership.

"You can buy a man's time, you can buy a man's physical presence at a certain place, you can even buy a measured number of skilled muscular motions per hour or day. But you cannot buy enthusiasm... you cannot buy loyalty; you cannot buy the devotion of hearts, minds, and souls. You have to earn these things."

—Clarence Francis

Don't take influence lightly.

In an age of social media, when people seek clicks to boost their numbers, develop your influence for a positive purpose. Influence people so that you can lead them—not for your benefit, but theirs. And for the team. **Lead people where they need to go so that they can accomplish their dreams.**

"Half of the harm that is done
in this world is due to people
who want to feel important.
They don't mean to do harm…
they are absorbed in
the endless struggle to think
well of themselves."

—T. S. Eliot

The bottom line is that an opportunity to lead people is an invitation to make a difference. Good leadership changes individual lives. It forms teams. It builds organizations. It impacts communities. It has the potential to impact the world. But never forget that influence is a responsibility. **Use it wisely.**

> # "LEADERSHIP IS AN OPPORTUNITY TO SERVE."

—J. Donald Walters

STEP

1

PROVE
YOURSELF

Can you influence others without accomplishing anything yourself? Yes, to a degree. You can *interest* them. You can make them your fans. You can get them to like you.

But can you take them anywhere? If people do nothing more than click Like, can you lead them where they need or want to go?

Probably not.

Leadership is influence,
but not all influence is leadership.

Influence without action isn't leadership.

The ability to produce results has always been the separation line for success. It is also a qualifying line for leadership. It creates credibility.

That's true in any community. **If you can produce results, you prove yourself. And you start to develop influence.**

"THERE ARE TWO TYPES OF PEOPLE IN THE BUSINESS COMMUNITY: THOSE WHO PRODUCE RESULTS AND THOSE WHO GIVE YOU REASONS WHY THEY DIDN'T."

—Peter Drucker

To prove yourself, don't worry about your position or status.

Stop asking yourself:

> **What are my rights?**
> **Is my authority clear?**
> **Where am I on the organizational chart?**
> **How do I compare to others?**
> **How can I climb the ladder?**
> **Who do I need to know?**
> **What's the next step in my career path?**

Forget about all that. Instead, get to work.

You can't fake productivity. Either you're producing for your team and adding to its bottom line (whatever that may be), or you're not.

Does *producer* describe you? Are you self-motivated and productive? Do you make your team better, stronger? Do you help create momentum? Do you help create an environment of success?

If you're a positive asset, people will respect you.

"THE OUTSTANDING LEADERS OF EVERY AGE ARE THOSE WHO SET UP THEIR OWN QUOTAS AND CONSTANTLY EXCEED THEM."

—Thomas Watson

SET THE BAR HIGH FOR YOURSELF

- Be successful *before* you try to help others be successful.
- Hold yourself to a higher standard than you ask of others.
- Make yourself accountable to others.
- Set tangible goals and then work to reach them.
- Accept responsibility for personal results.
- Admit failures and mistakes quickly and humbly.
- Ask from others only what you have previously asked of yourself.
- Measure your success by results, not intentions.
- Remove yourself from situations where you are ineffective.

TO PROVE YOURSELF, KNOW YOURSELF

Human nature seems to endow people with the ability to size up everybody in the world but themselves. So, what are you to do? Become a student of yourself.

Self-knowledge is foundational for being productive and influencing others.

What are your strengths and weaknesses? What is your temperament? What are your work habits, your daily, monthly, and seasonal rhythms?

If you're not sure about these things, ask others who know you and who will be honest with you.

"Hard experience has taught me that real leadership is about understanding yourself first, then using that to create a superb organization... Most obstacles that limit people's potential are set in motion by the leader and are rooted in his or her own fears, ego needs, and unproductive habits. When leaders explore deep within their thoughts and feelings in order to understand themselves, a transformation can take shape."

—D. Michael Abrashoff

It's very difficult to be self-deluded and successful at the same time. You will be productive and prove yourself only if you see yourself clearly, acknowledge your weaknesses, and work in your strengths.

To prove yourself, you must be yourself.
To be yourself, you must know yourself.

"LOOKING BACK, MY LIFE SEEMS LIKE ONE LONG OBSTACLE RACE, WITH ME AS ITS CHIEF OBSTACLE."

—Jack Paar

KNOW YOUR VALUES

Your values will become the soul of your leadership.
They inform how you interact with others. They drive your
behavior. Before you seek to influence others, gain a clear
understanding of your values and commit to living them
consistently.

What are your...

> **Ethical Values:** How do you define right and wrong, and
> what lines will you never cross?
> **Relational Values:** How will you treat people, and what
> behaviors are out-of-bounds?
> **Success Values:** How do you define success, and what won't
> you do to achieve it?

If you know your values and live by them,
you can work and lead with integrity.

TO PROVE YOURSELF, IMPROVE YOURSELF

There are many things you *can't* change about yourself. Where and when you were born. How you were raised. Your height. Your natural wiring.

Accept them.

There are lots of things you *can* change about yourself. Work hard to improve them.

"He who has so little knowledge
of human nature as to seek happiness
by changing anything
but his own disposition will waste
his life in fruitless efforts
and multiply the grief which
he purposes to remove."

—Samuel Johnson

Too often we look outside of ourselves
for the source of our problems.
The reality is that many come from inside us.
Work on those.

BE THE KIND OF PERSON OTHERS WANT TO FOLLOW

In a survey by Opinion Research Corporation for Ajilon Finance, American workers were asked to select the one trait that was most important to them in a leader.

RANK	CHARACTERISTIC	PERCENTAGE
1	Leading by Example	26%
2	Strong Ethics or Morals	19%
3	Knowledge of the Business	17%
4	Fairness	14%
5	Overall Intelligence and Competence	13%
6	Recognition of Employees	10%

The good news is that these are choices you can make as a leader. You can *choose* to be a good example. You can *choose* to embrace ethics and have good morals. You can *choose* to learn the business. You can *choose* to be fair. You can *choose* to improve your competence and even to increase your intelligence. You can *choose* to recognize the people you work with.

Make these choices, and people will respect you and begin to follow you.

HOW WILL YOUR LEADERSHIP LOOK?

As you do your work and prepare to lead others, think about what kinds of habits and systems you will consistently practice. What will you do to organize yourself? How will you start your day when you arrive at work? What spiritual practices will you maintain to keep yourself on track? How will you treat people? What will be your work ethic? What kind of example will you set?

You determine what kind of person and leader you will be. It's up to you to define yourself. The earlier you are in your career, the greater your potential to positively influence others by doing the right things in the right ways.

"My best lesson in leadership came during my early days as a trial lawyer. Wanting to learn from the best, I went to see two of the most renowned litigators in San Antonio try cases. One sat there and never objected to anything, was very gentle with witnesses, and established a rapport with the jury. The other was an aggressive, thundering hell-raiser. And both seemed to win every case. That's when I realized there are many different paths, not one right path. That's true of leadership as well. People with different personalities, different approaches, or different values succeed not because one set of values or practices is superior, but because their values and practices are *genuine*."

—Herb Kelleher

As you gain influence, how will you use it? As people begin to follow you, what kind of leader will you be? **You can develop whatever style of leadership you want as long as it benefits others and is consistent with who you are.**

"Leadership is much less about what you *do*,
and much more about who you *are*.
If you view leadership as a bag of manipulative
tricks or charismatic behaviors to advance
your own personal interest, then people have
every right to be cynical. But if your leadership
flows first and foremost from inner character
and integrity of ambition, then you can
justly ask people to lend themselves
to your organization and its mission."

—Frances Hesselbein

Begin acting like the kind of leader
you would be glad to follow.

STEP

2

EARN

RELATIONSHIPS

"You can impress people from a distance, but you must get close to influence them... The most essential quality for leadership is not perfection but credibility. People must be able to trust you."

—Rick Warren

Building relationships with people is the next step in developing influence. When people feel liked, cared for, included, valued, and trusted, they gladly work together with their leader and each other.

You can change an entire working environment by building relationships.

Relationships can break down organizational silos as people make connections across established lines. They think less about job descriptions or departments and more about other people. As more barriers come down and relationships deepen, trust grows. That foundation of trust changes the way people work together. And how they interact with their leaders.

The old saying is really true: People go along with people they get along with.

Being relational is a risk, just as it is risky when you open yourself up to falling in love.

Sure, you can stay guarded and never get hurt. But you will also never have the chance to develop deep, rewarding work relationships that will enrich your life and the lives of others.

To achieve anything worthwhile in life, you need to leave your comfort zone. That involves taking risks, which can be frightening. However, each time you leave your comfort zone and conquer new territory, it not only expands your comfort zone but also enlarges you.

If you want to grow as an influencer, be prepared to be uncomfortable. Extend yourself to others.

Take the risk. Choose to build relationships. Yes, occasionally people will take advantage of you. Yes, you may be hurt. But the benefits far outweigh the risks.

If you respect people, trust them, and treat them well, most of them will respond the same way to you.

If in the past you have relied on rules and procedures to get things done or keep things going, now is the time to change your focus. Instead, do what it takes to earn relationships with people. Why? Because the reality is that *people* get things done, not the playbook they use.

- Where you once thought in terms of procedures, think more in terms of people's emotions.

- Where you once focused on production capacity, think more in terms of human capacity.

- Where you once considered the bottom line, think more in terms of people's potential.

In other words, always think of people first
before you try to achieve progress.

People are the power behind any team
or organization. Focus on them.
Use a personal touch whenever you can.

**Listen,
learn,
and then
lead.**

Earning relationships is possible only when you respect and value people. It is impossible to relate well with those you don't respect.

You can care for people without leading them, but you cannot lead them well without caring for them.

"KIND WORDS CAN BE SHORT
AND EASY TO SPEAK,
BUT THEIR ECHOES
ARE TRULY ENDLESS."

—Mother Teresa

If you are not a people person, it may take you some time to develop people skills. But it doesn't have to take any time for you to let others know you value them. Express appreciation for them, and take an interest in them personally. You can do that now. Today.

The moment people notice a positive shift in your attitude toward them, they will start responding positively to you. That can lay the cornerstone upon which you start building positive relationships.

"Do you know how I identify
someone who needs encouragement?
If the person is breathing,
they need a pat on the back!"

—S. Truett Cathy

INFLUENCERS ARE INITIATORS

Take responsibility for reaching out to the people on your team. Don't wait for them to come to you. Do what you must to connect with them.

If you want to earn relationships, break up your routine. Get out of your own territory. Move beyond your job description, both in terms of the work you do and the way you interact with people.

"LET HIM THAT WOULD MOVE
THE WORLD FIRST MOVE HIMSELF."

—Socrates

Learn who your team members are.

Discover their aspirations. Find out what they need.
Get to know them as individuals.

Everyone on your team has hopes, dreams, desires, and goals of their own. Ask about them.

Your job is to try to align your team members' aspirations with the organization's vision in a way that benefits everyone.

You may be tempted to build relationships only with the people you automatically like or with whom you are highly compatible. You may want to ignore the others.

Don't make that mistake!

It's difficult to help anyone you don't influence.
Why give up that opportunity?

Instead, make the effort. If you try to connect with people, there's always a *chance* you can build a positive relationship. **If you don't try, there is no chance.**

Will it be harder to connect with someone you don't like? Yes. While it's true that the things we have in common with others make relationships easy and enjoyable, the differences make them **interesting**.

TAKE STEPS FORWARD TO BUILD RELATIONSHIPS

- Make a choice to care about others. Liking people and caring about them are choices within your control. If you haven't already, make that choice.

- Look for something that is likeable about every person on your team. It's there. Make it your job to find it.

- Discover what is likeable about yourself and do whatever you can to share that with every person you meet. That's the start of adding value to others.

- Make the effort every day to express what you like about every person on your team.

NEVER DEVALUE ANYONE

No matter how frustrated you get, how often people make mistakes, or how difficult they can be, never devalue people...

By not having a genuine belief in them.

By assuming they *can't* instead of assuming they *can*.

By assuming they *won't* rather than believing they *will*.

By seeing their *problems* more readily than their *potential*.

By viewing them as *liabilities* instead of *assets*.

Your job as a leader is to *add value*.

Treat everyone as you want to be treated.
Better yet, treat them the way
they want to be treated.

EARN THEIR TRUST

Trust is the foundation of all positive relationships.

Trust is required for people to feel safe enough to create, share, question, attempt, and risk. Without trust, influence is weak and teamwork is impossible. They are afraid to be themselves.

If you have integrity with people in every situation, they will develop trust in you. The more trust you develop, the stronger the relationship can become. The stronger the relationship, the greater the potential for gaining influence. It's a building process that takes time, energy, and intentionality.

"WHEN THE CRUNCH COMES,
PEOPLE CLING TO THOSE
THEY KNOW THEY CAN TRUST."

—James Stockdale

In times of difficulty,
relationships are a shelter.

In times of opportunity,
relationships are a launching pad.

To develop authentic relationships, you must be authentic. Own up to your faults. Recognize your shortcomings. Admit your mistakes. Apologize.

In other words, you must be the real deal.

That is a vulnerable place to be. It is one of the main reasons people in leadership positions don't earn relationships and develop greater influence. They are afraid to be themselves.

Most people don't want to admit their mistakes, expose their faults, and face up to their shortcomings.

They don't want to be exposed. Discovered.

Don't hide in times of trouble.

You can't maintain a facade with the people you lead and build authentic relationships. Be honest and humble to develop trust. Exhibit a consistent mood, maintain an optimistic attitude, possess a listening ear, and present your authentic self to others.

"You see, when there is danger, a good leader takes the front line; but when there is celebration, a good leader stays in the back room… If you want the cooperation of humans around you, you must make them feel they are important— and you do that by being genuine and humble."

—Nelson Mandela

Being relational doesn't mean ignoring problems or being unrealistic about people.

You must still look at hard truths, see people's flaws, and face reality. But you can do those things in a spirit of grace and truth.

Conflict is a part of progress for anyone who wants to lead others.

Use your influence to help people when conflict arises.
Don't avoid people's problems; help people *solve* their problems. That's what influence is for.

YOU CAN'T EXPECT TO GET
A CROP WITHOUT PLOWING,
AND YOU CAN'T EXPECT RAIN
WITHOUT THUNDER AND LIGHTNING.

—Frederick Douglass (paraphrased)

Developing good relationships creates energy and produces a positive environment for a team. When you invest time and effort to get to know people and build relationships, in the long run it will produce greater energy than it takes from you.

In that kind of positive, energetic environment, people are willing to give their best because they know their leader cares about them and wants the best for them.

RELATIONAL INFLUENCERS

HOW THEY THINK
Side by Side

WHAT THEY SAY
"Let's work together."

HOW THEY THINK
Initiation

WHAT THEY SAY
"I'll come to you."

HOW THEY THINK
Inclusion

WHAT THEY SAY
"What do you think?"

HOW THEY THINK
Cooperation

WHAT THEY SAY
"Together we can win."

HOW THEY THINK
Service

WHAT THEY SAY
"I'm here to help you."

HOW THEY THINK
Development

WHAT THEY SAY
"I want to add value to you."

HOW THEY THINK
Encouragement

WHAT THEY SAY
"I believe you can do this!"

HOW THEY THINK
Innovation

WHAT THEY SAY
"Let's think outside the box."

STEP

3

MAKE

YOUR TEAM

SUCCESSFUL

If you can be productive as a person *and* help your team become productive and successful, your influence will grow to new heights.

Being able to make the team successful is a qualifying mark of leadership.

Developing a group of people into a productive team is no easy task. You may find it challenging to get everybody working together to achieve a common vision. But what is the alternative? People doing their own thing, going their own way, the group never working together to accomplish anything significant?

Being part of a team of people doing something of high value is one of the most rewarding experiences in life. As a leader with influence, you have a chance to help people experience it. Don't shrink back from that great opportunity.

A good team is always greater than the sum of its parts and is able to accomplish more than individuals working alone. It takes someone with influence to get those parts to work together.

"You can issue all the memos and give all the motivational speeches you want, but if the rest of the people in your organization don't see you putting forth your very best effort every single day, they won't either."

—Colin Powell

BE THE MODEL

To influence team members toward success, you must show the way to productivity. People always believe what we do more than what we say. Your credibility as a team leader can be summed up in one word: *example*.

Lead by example and deliver results yourself.
Show people the way forward. Your performance opens the way
for their potential.

Let results silence your critics and build your reputation.

"Don't worry about making friends;
don't worry about making enemies.
Worry about winning, because
if you win, your enemies
can't hurt you, and if you lose,
your friends can't stand you."

—Paul "Bear" Bryant

When you are capable and productive,
you *take* your teammates along
to where you want them to go—
you don't *send* them there.

As your influence on the team increases, people will start seeing you as a leader. When that happens, the responsibility for your team's success will rest on your shoulders. You must be willing to bear that weight as you work to help your team succeed.

Productivity is measurable. You must help your team achieve it. Organizational growth is tangible. You must help your team increase it. Profitability is quantifiable. You must help your team improve it.

High performance requires high commitment.

WHERE DO YOU FIT IN?

One of the keys to making your team successful is understanding how your gifts and abilities can be used to help others be productive and further the mission of the team.

How can you use your talents and skills to make everyone else on the team successful?

"Do [what you do] so well that
when people see you do it,
they will want to come back
to see you do it again, and they will
want to bring others and show them
how well you do what you do."

—Walt Disney

Don't allow yourself to become the lid on your team.
Don't hold people back. Don't try to do everything yourself.
**Find ways to engage their talent and empower them
to be successful.**

"People and organizations don't grow much without delegation and completed staff work because they are confined to the capacities of the boss and reflect both personal strengths and weaknesses."

—Stephen Covey

HELP YOUR TEAM SOLVE PROBLEMS

Few things garner influence faster than the ability to solve problems.

Become your team's catalyst for problem-solving. Rally everyone to break through obstacles, put out fires, and correct mistakes. Find better ways to do things together. Harness the power of the team to keep getting better.

"NOTHING BUILDS SELF-ESTEEM
AND SELF-CONFIDENCE
LIKE ACCOMPLISHMENT."

—Thomas Carlyle

Productivity is inspiring.

People who feel good about themselves often produce good results.
And good results create positive momentum and high morale.

> "BE WILLING TO MAKE DECISIONS.
> THAT'S THE MOST IMPORTANT QUALITY
> IN A GOOD LEADER."
>
> —George S. Patton

"BE WILLING TO MAKE DECISIONS.
THAT'S THE MOST IMPORTANT QUALITY
IN A GOOD LEADER."

—George S. Patton

LEADERS ARE WILLING TO MAKE DIFFICULT DECISIONS

Whenever you see winning teams or thriving organizations, you can be sure their leaders made some very tough decisions—and are continuing to make them.

When you make tough decisions for the team,
you gain respect.

When those decisions are the right decisions,
you gain influence.

Success is an uphill journey.

No team ever coasted its way to victory. If you have the privilege of leading your team, you will have to make tough decisions for everyone's benefit.

You are more likely to regret the decisions you failed to make than the decisions you made that didn't work.

As a leader, if you continually neglect making necessary decisions, your influence will diminish. Your team will stop trusting you. And eventually, they will no longer follow.

WHEN YOU HELP YOUR TEAM SUCCEED...

GOOD PEOPLE WANT TO JOIN YOU

When your team is winning, it attracts other highly productive people. Winners attract winners. Producers attract producers. They respect one another. They enjoy collaborating. They get things done together.

EVERYONE BECOMES MOTIVATED

Few things inspire people like victory. The job of a leader is to help the team succeed. As individuals on the team get to experience successes, they become motivated to keep going and reach for larger successes.

Reward and celebrate small victories. Acknowledge team members and give them the credit they deserve. Not only will that motivate them but it will also help them enjoy the journey.

MORALE INCREASES

Which comes first, high morale or high productivity? That's a chicken-or-egg question. But this is certain: If production goes down, morale will fade fast. **Keep producing, and high morale continues.**

"Morale is a state of mind.
It is a steadfastness and courage
and hope. It is confidence and zeal
and loyalty... It is staying power,
the spirit which endures to the end—
the will to win. With it all things are
possible; without it everything else...
count[s] for naught."

—George C. Marshall

HELP TEAM MEMBERS PLAY TO THEIR STRENGTHS

Author Jim Collins writes about the importance of getting the right people in the right seats on the bus.

Successful leaders help their people find their right seats.

Don't be afraid to move people around to find where they make the greatest contribution. Sometimes it means trying and failing. Positioning people well is a process, and you have to treat it that way. You will never help people reach their potential or create a winning team until people are doing what they do best.

Make it your goal to help every person spend most of their time on their should-dos and love-to-dos.

"Most of us lead busy but undisciplined lives. We have ever-expanding 'to do' lists, trying to build momentum by doing, doing, doing— and doing more. And it rarely works. Those who build the good-to-great companies, however, made as much use of 'stop doing' lists as 'to do' lists. They displayed a remarkable discipline to unplug all sorts of extraneous junk."

—Jim Collins

COMMUNICATE THE MISSION

Do your team members know and understand the mission? How do you know that they know?

Never take anything for granted. Communicate the mission often. Make sure team members understand how their talents and efforts are supposed to contribute to it.

GET TEAM MEMBERS TO WORK TOGETHER

As a leader, your job is to influence people to work together. Help them bring their strengths to make the team better. Help them compensate for each other's weaknesses.

Of course, this implies that you *know* their strengths and weaknesses. Is that true? Have you connected with every team member to get to know them?

"THE JOB OF A LEADER IS TO BUILD A COMPLEMENTARY TEAM, WHERE EVERY STRENGTH IS MADE EFFECTIVE AND EACH WEAKNESS IS MADE IRRELEVANT."

—Stephen Covey

CREATE AN ENVIRONMENT CONDUCIVE TO GROWTH AND INSPIRATION

When you have influence, you set the environment for your team. Make it your goal to lift up everyone and help them do their best.

Your attitude is contagious. When you are positive, encouraging, and open to growth, your teammates will be too.

"Hereafter, if you should observe on occasion to give your officers and friends a little more praise than is their Due, and confess more fault than you can justly be charged with, you will only become the sooner for it a Great Captain. Criticising and censuring almost every one you have to do with, will diminish friends, encrease Enemies, and thereby hurt your affairs."

—Benjamin Franklin in a letter to John Paul Jones

GIVE TEAM MEMBERS CONSTRUCTIVE FEEDBACK

People always want to know how they're doing. They want to succeed, and if they're not succeeding, they usually want to know how to make adjustments to improve.

As a leader, you are in the best position to give them that feedback. Do that well, and you increase your influence.

Most people are willing to change if they are convinced that changing will help them win. Walk your team members through that process.

YOUR TEAM'S CONTINUED SUCCESS IS YOUR SUCCESS

What's the bottom line when it comes to working with a team?
Results.

To successfully influence your team, you need to help
the people on it achieve results.

Results always matter—regardless of how many obstacles you face, what the economy does, what kinds of problems your team members create, or how difficult the task. **Keep fighting for productivity.**

**And keep fighting,
even when you experience success!**

"More men are failures on account of success than on account of failures. They beat their way over a dozen obstacles, overcome a host of difficulties, sacrifice and sweat. They make the impossible the possible; then along comes a little success, and it tumbles them from their perch. They let up, they slip and over they go. Nobody can count the number of people who have been halted and beaten by recognition and reward!"

—Henry Ford

Keep taking the team forward. If your team gains momentum, don't back off. Press on and increase the momentum so that the team can accomplish even greater things.

The longer you help your team remain focused and productive, the greater success your team members will experience. The greater success they experience, the more influence you will have with them.

STEP
4

HELP PEOPLE REACH THEIR POTENTIAL

PEOPLE ARE AN ORGANIZATION'S MOST APPRECIABLE ASSET

Most of what an organization possesses goes down in value. Facilities deteriorate. Equipment becomes obsolete. Supplies get used up.

People appreciate—but only if they are valued, challenged, and developed by someone capable of investing in them and helping them grow.

People don't appreciate automatically or grow accidentally.
Growth occurs in people only when someone intentionally invests in them.

Otherwise, they are like money put on deposit without interest. Their potential is high, but they aren't actually growing.

If you have helped people become successful as part of a team, you will have enough influence to move forward to step four. People will welcome your desire to invest in them.

If you are highly successful and have a lot to give, they will be blown away by your desire to give it.

If you want to go to a higher level of influence with people, you need to think beyond productivity and team success and start thinking in terms of how you can help individuals on your team to improve themselves and tap into their potential.

Do this with no strings attached, and you will help change people's lives!

No leader is self-made. No successful person makes it on their own.

What you have received from others was their gift to you. Your gift back is to help others in any way you can to make them successful and teach them how to become leaders.

That's how to make a positive difference in the world.

Few things in life are better than seeing people reach their potential. If you help people become better on the inside, eventually they will become greater on the outside.

People are like trees: Give them what they need to grow on a continual basis for long enough, and they will grow from the inside out.

And they will bear fruit.

Invest in people, and they will
never be the same again.

Neither will you.

It is impossible to help others
without helping yourself.

HOW TO START HELPING PEOPLE REACH THEIR POTENTIAL

Shift your focus from people's production to their potential.

As you work with someone, spend 20 percent of your time helping them with their personal productivity. Spend 80 percent of your time helping them develop as a person.

This can be difficult if you are a highly productive person. You may want to focus entirely on training skills. But in the long run, it's more important to help people change and grow as individuals.

Help someone become a better person, and *everything* in their life improves.

"A LEADER'S ROLE IS NOT
TO CONTROL PEOPLE
OR STAY ON TOP OF THINGS,
BUT RATHER TO GUIDE,
ENERGIZE, AND EXCITE."

—Jack Welch

Who should you develop? Start with the people with the greatest potential. That may go against your instincts. Most people root for the underdog. But picking the person you think can go the furthest with your help is more effective.

Think of this as the "put on your own oxygen mask first" principle. If you've heard the safety message on a plane, you know the more capable person is to put on their own oxygen mask first before helping someone else.

If you help the more capable people
to develop and improve first,
then they can join you
in helping other people.

"When you look at people who are eager to learn more, you can bet they are on the right track. And when you talk to people who just don't want any more instruction, then they have pretty much hit the wall. They are done."

—James H. Blanchard

If you want the best for your team or organization, invest in people. In a competitive business world, the ability to develop people often makes the difference between two organizations competing to succeed using similar resources.

Changing your focus to people development does more than help the person you develop. **It can revolutionize an organization and give it a much brighter future.**

Organizations get better
when their people get better.
That's why investing in people always
gives the greatest return.

"IF YOU ARE SUCCESSFUL,
IT IS BECAUSE SOMEWHERE,
SOMETIME, SOMEONE
GAVE YOU A LIFE OR AN IDEA
THAT STARTED YOU IN
THE RIGHT DIRECTION."

—Melinda Gates

QUALITIES OF
A DEVELOPER

Authenticity—This is the foundation for developing people.

Servanthood—This is the soul for developing people.

Growth—This is the measurement for developing people.

Excellence—This is the standard for developing people.

Passion—This is the fuel for developing people.

Success—This is the purpose for developing people.

"[If employers fail to upgrade their workers,] then they're trying to be competitive only with their capital. Anybody can replicate physical capital. But the one [resource] nobody can replicate is the dedication, the teamwork, the skills of a company's employees."

—Robert Reich

Nobody gets ahead in life without the help and support of other people. One of the great privileges of investing in people to develop their potential is helping them navigate through life's difficulties.

It's difficult for someone to make the most of their potential when the rest of their life is a wreck. Helping people develop good life skills helps them create a strong foundation upon which to build a family, a career, and a spiritual life.

You will receive joy when you know that you've helped someone to enjoy life and live it well.

Meet regularly with people you're investing in. Mentor them.

Give them advice and opportunities to grow and learn.

"The purpose of life is not to win.
The purpose in life is to grow
and to share. When you come to look
back on all that you have done in life,
you will get more satisfaction from
the pleasure you have brought into
other people's lives than you will
from the times that you outdid
and defeated them."

—Rabbi Harold Kushner

DON'T LET SELF-CENTEREDNESS KEEP YOU FROM DEVELOPING PEOPLE

Maturity gives you the ability to think beyond yourself, see things from the perspective of others, and place their needs above your own. **Maturity will serve you well as you help people reach their potential.**

Its opposite isn't immaturity. It's selfishness.

"WHEN YOU BECOME A LEADER
YOU GIVE UP THE RIGHT
TO THINK ABOUT YOURSELF."

—Gerald Brooks

When you have influence, you have the authority to serve people in new ways. You also have the responsibility. You won't do that if you have a self-serving attitude.

DON'T LET INSECURITY KEEP YOU FROM DEVELOPING PEOPLE

The best leaders are willing to work themselves out of their job. They are not insecure. Rather than worrying that someone they train and develop will take their job, a good leader hopes that person becomes strong enough to do their job so that they can move on to something else.

"NO AMOUNT OF
PERSONAL COMPETENCY
CAN COMPENSATE FOR
PERSONAL INSECURITY."

—Wayne Schmidt

Don't worry about your position and standing. Learn not to feel threatened. The best way to ensure that you have a bright future is to keep growing yourself as you invest in others. That way you will never run out of something to give. And you will always be preparing yourself for something better.

DON'T LET SHORTSIGHTEDNESS KEEP YOU FROM DEVELOPING PEOPLE

How many times have you considered giving someone a task that would help them to grow and learn but instead thought, "It's easier to just do it myself"?

Why would anyone think that way?

Because it *is* easier.

Doing work yourself is always faster and easier than developing other people to do it. But that's short-term thinking!

To become someone who helps others reach their potential, you have to be willing to adopt a long-term mindset. You must be willing to pay the price on the front end. The return comes on the back end when the person has been developed. That's when you win, the team wins, and the person you developed wins.

Investing in people takes a lot of time and energy. It takes patience. Shortsightedness, like selfishness and insecurity, is a sign of immaturity.

Keep the big picture in mind and invest in people.
Otherwise, you limit the potential of yourself, your people, and your organization.

Bringing out the best in a person
is often a catalyst for bringing out
the best in the team.

If you've ever looked around and thought, "How do we meet so many needs in these troubled times?" then realize that the greatest needs will never be met until we equip leaders who can work to meet those needs.

This is a cause worthy of a lifetime commitment.

The highest investment you can make
in another person—and the most influential—
is giving your time, energy, money,
and thinking to helping them become
a good leader.

"Making the right people decisions is the ultimate means of controlling an organization well. Such decisions reveal how competent management is, what its values are, and whether it takes its job seriously. No matter how hard managers try to keep their decisions a secret—and some still try hard—people decisions cannot be hidden. They are eminently visible... Executives who do not make the effort to get their people decisions right do more than risk poor performance. They risk losing their organization's respect."

—Peter Drucker

When you look for someone to develop as a leader, don't look at their title, position, age, gender, or experience. Gauge their potential to influence others and their ability to learn and grow.

Very few people are both able and willing to develop others to become leaders.

Attracting, developing, and leading other leaders is much more difficult than leading followers. That's why so few people do it.

Don't settle for *influencing followers*.
Use your influence to *develop leaders*.

Only leaders can develop other people to become leaders.

A well-intentioned person lacking leadership knowledge and experience cannot train another person to lead.

Theorists who study leadership without practicing it cannot equip someone to lead, just as a cookbook reader with no experience in the kitchen cannot teach someone else to cook.

People don't really understand leading until they do it. That's why it's so important for you to develop leaders.

**The more influence you have,
the more you need to pass it on to others
who can make a difference.**

It takes a leader to KNOW a leader.

Only a leader can recruit and position potential leaders.

It takes a leader to SHOW a leader.

Only a leader can model leadership and equip others to lead.

It takes a leader to GROW a leader.

Only a leader can develop and empower others
to be leaders—and measure their progress.

"The best executive is
the one who has sense enough
to pick good men to do what
he wants done, and self-restraint
enough to keep from meddling
with them while they do it."

—Theodore Roosevelt

What Roosevelt is describing is empowerment.

Your ultimate goal is to help people learn and see what they can do without your help.

But you need to help them get there.

STAGES OF LEADERSHIP

The Center for Organizational Leadership in Cincinnati, Ohio, identifies six degrees of ability based on how independently a team member can work.

As you help people learn to lead, keep in mind what stage is appropriate for them before moving them on to the next.

At each stage, you can ask them to:

1. Look into it. Report back. You'll decide what to do.
2. Look into it. Report alternatives with pros and cons and their recommendation.
3. Look into it. Let you know what they intend to do, but don't do it unless you say yes.
4. Look into it. Let you know what they intend to do, and do it unless you say no.
5. Take action. Let you know what they did.
6. Take action. No further contact with you is required.

Your ultimate goal is to help them become leaders who can take action without needing your help or input.

Teach people to lead in their own right.

Few things put wind in another person's sails like your faith in them.

To empower people, you must have genuine faith in them.
You can't fake it. You can't borrow someone else's belief in a person.
It must be genuine.

As you develop people, use the positive experiences you've had with them to fuel your faith in them. Reinforce your belief by remembering the growth they've already achieved. Underline that belief with success they have already exhibited. Speak positive belief into them.

People rise to their leader's level of expectations.

The greatest satisfaction in life comes from giving to others.

You will be most fulfilled when you forget advancing yourself and focus on developing others.

You will find that you are closest to the people you help to grow to their potential.

When the giving that comes from developing people is added to the solid relationships you've built with them and the success you've helped them achieve, you will discover the richest experiences of your life.

You will be using your influence for the greatest good you can achieve. You will experience significance.

Once you've tasted significance,
success will never satisfy you again.

WITH GREAT
INFLUENCE
COMES GREAT
RESPONSIBILITY

THE INFLUENCE FORMULA

This is the influence formula.

- Prove yourself.

- Earn relationships.

- Make your team successful.

- Help people reach their potential.

It is your best pathway for developing
as a leader and being able to help people
and work with a team.

Will everyone follow you if you follow this formula?
The answer is no.

You have no control over another person's response to you. Some people will ignore the good work you do. Some will resist allowing you to develop a relationship with them. All you can do is keep trying. You can keep adding value to them. You can keep working to help them succeed. In time, they may come around. But that's their choice, not yours.

If you are gaining in influence, use it wisely—not for personal gain but for the betterment of others. To whom much is given, much shall be required.

Use the power of your influence to add value to people and make the world a better place.

"MOST PEOPLE CAN BEAR ADVERSITY.
BUT IF YOU WISH TO KNOW WHAT
A MAN REALLY IS; GIVE HIM POWER.
THIS IS THE SUPREME TEST."

—Robert G. Ingersoll

How can you tell if you have used your influence wisely? Consider what happens when you meet with your team.

- Do your team members share their thoughts and ideas freely?

- Are the best ideas rarely your ideas?

- If you contribute ideas, does the discussion quickly move from your idea to the best idea?

- Are you happy when that happens?

How about when your team performs?

- When your team succeeds, do your team members get the majority of the credit?

- Is there a shared sense of pride in the work that's being done?

- When things go wrong, do you personally accept the greatest share of the blame?

If you're using your influence wisely, your team will be rising up and receiving recognition and you will be working in the background to make them more successful.

"Victory is much more meaningful when it comes not just from one person, but from the joint achievements of many. The euphoria is lasting when all participants lead with their hearts, winning not just for themselves but for one another."

—Howard Schultz

Your ultimate goal for gaining influence should be for others. Help them to come together, work together, and win at something worthwhile.

Influence whomever you can for good.
Make the world a better place.

ACKNOWLEDGMENTS

I want to say thank you to Charlie Wetzel and the rest of the team who assisted me with the formation and publication of this book. And to the people in my organizations who support it. You all add incredible value to me, which allows me to add value to others. Together, we're making a difference!